Thanks!

From

WCL Board
8/23/2012

Oh, Thank Goodness, It's Not Just Me!

Woman *to* Woman
… Heart *to* Heart

LISA HAMMOND *and* **BJ GALLAGHER**

simple truths®

Published by SimpleTruths, LLC
1952 McDowell Road, Suite 205
Naperville, Illinois 60563

Design and production: Koechel Peterson & Associates, Inc., Minneapolis, MN

Edited by: Stephanie Trannel

Simple Truths is a registered trademark.

Printed and bound in the United States of America

ISBN 978-1-60810-067-5

800-900-3427
www.simpletruths.com

01 WOZ 10

Table of Contents

Friendship is born at that moment

when one person says to another, "What! You, too?

I thought I was the only one!"

C.S. Lewis, British author

Introduction

I HAVE ALWAYS been considered a bit of a loud mouth—both literally and figuratively. My candor is refreshing to some—too frank for others. Regardless, I have always been a tell-it-like-it-is kind of gal. Over the years, I have found my candid approach to life resonates more with women than with men.

Sometimes, after I have shared a personal story during a speech or workshop, women approach me, expressing a deep sense of gratitude for my willingness to reveal my warts and all. The discovery that they were not alone in their imperfections was like water on dry ground for these women. You could almost hear their collective sighs of relief, *You mean I am not the only one?*

Recently I was at a party where—as usual—the women all gravitated to one area, talking together. Some were mothers; others were not.

One of the young moms had her small children with her. She looked exhausted as she tried to get her infant to sleep while trying to keep her toddler from escaping.

I told her that I barely stayed sane when my kids were that age—I was proud of myself if I managed to shower before the sun went down! She practically had tears in her eyes as she listened to my admission. I told her, "Since starting my own business, I can tell you—with all sincerity—that an 18-hour day at the office is a walk in the park compared to a day at home with small children! Being a mom is the hardest job on the planet."

She blinked back tears as she said, "I thought it was just me! All of the other moms at the mall always look so happy pushing their strollers up and down the aisles."

I told her, "They are probably at the mall to keep themselves from going crazy at home—feeling just like you are."

"I never thought about it that way," she replied. "I thought I was the only one that was miserable and that all the other moms were so perfect. Thank you!"

Women today face more challenges than ever—accompanied by feelings of being overwhelmed and spread much too thin. More and more of us are raising our hands and speaking up, telling the truth about how we feel. And as we do, other women are saying, "Me, too! Oh, thank God I'm not the only one!"

As we become more open and honest with each other—more willing to admit maybe we don't love being a mother every single day—maybe we can't remember the last time we actually had time to shave our legs—maybe our white picket fence life didn't turn out the way we thought it would—maybe we aren't rock stars at work every single day—maybe it is okay to say we are each doing the best we can—even if sometimes the best we can do is mediocre.

Slowly we are starting to realize we are not alone. This book is a celebration of the circle of strength women share— the common experiences in all our lives. The undeniable fact is that there is comfort and reassurance in knowing we are not alone.

~ Lisa Hammond, the "Barefoot CEO" of Femail Creations

{ SECTION I }

We fear that
we're all alone.

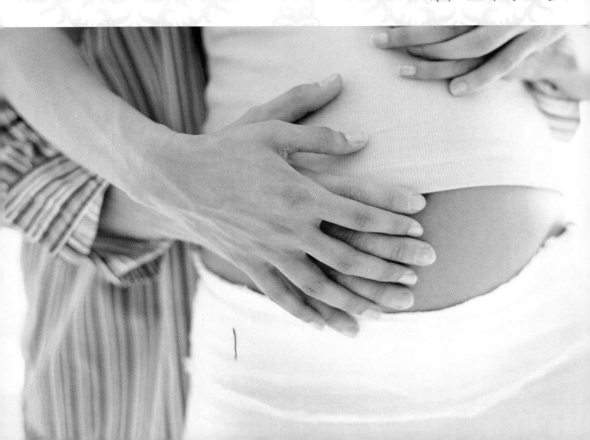

"The deepest need of man is the need to overcome his separateness, to leave the prison of his aloneness."

Erich Fromm, psychoanalyst, philosopher

ERICH FROMM MAY HAVE used the generic "man" in his statement, but we all know that he was referring to women, too...and children. A sense of separateness is endemic to the human condition. Before birth, when you were inside your mother's womb, you were at one with your mother—indeed, with the entire universe. You felt connected—*you were connected*—in the most intimate way to another human being and to life itself. The comforting sound of mom's heartbeat kept you company 24/7. You were never alone.

Then your birthday came and it was time to leave the warm, wet, dark safety of mom's womb and come out into the bright light, where you opened your eyes, took a few gasping breaths, and perhaps let out a cry. With a quick snip, your umbilical cord was cut and that most intimate of connections was forever severed. Your life has never been the same.

Many people spend the rest of their lives feeling separate from others, even family members and dear friends. Some people report feeling "different" from others, profoundly lonely in their sense of isolation. Some even feel like "something's wrong with me" because of this lingering sense of separate-ness haunting them. "You're OK; *I'm not OK,*" they fear.

Psychologist Will Schutz said that deep down inside, we each have three basic fears: (1) the fear that we're incompe-tent, (2) the fear that we're insignificant or unworthy, and (3) the fear that we're unlovable. To these, we would add one more especially for women—the fear that we're crazy. These fears drive our behavior, even when we don't realize it.

Many of us go to great lengths to prove that these fears aren't true—we work hard to prove that we ARE competent, we ARE significant, and we ARE lovable—and that we're NOT crazy. But even when we "prove" it to others, we never quite prove it to ourselves. The fears linger. We are loathe to share things with others that might make us look bad, con-firming our worst suspicions about ourselves. These four deeply-held fears keep us isolated as prisoners of self-doubt, anxiety and self-criticism.

The first section of this book examines each of these fears—for it is only by shining the light of day on our fears that we see them for what they truly are:

False
Evidence
Appearing
Real

In overcoming fear and sharing our stories with
others, we find the truth about who we really are—and
discover that we're not alone.

We Fear We're Incompetent.

CHAPTER 1

SCIENTISTS ARE LEARNING more and more all the time about significant brain differences between men and women. Men are single-focused, while women excel at multi-tasking. Men need to use only about 14,000 words to feel fully self-expressed at the end of the day, while women need to use about 46,000 words to feel fully self-expressed. Men's brains are superior when it comes to spatial object relationships, while women's brains are superior in attending to the subtle cues of non-verbal communication. Each gender has its own areas of brain strength—and weakness. *Vive le difference!*

When things go wrong, men and women also react differently. As therapist Cathy Conheim explains, a woman looks first to herself as the source of the problem, "What's wrong with me that I can't __(fill in the blank)__?" It doesn't matter what the problem is—a woman will almost always blame herself. "What's wrong with me that I can't earn more money? What's wrong with me that my husband is unfaithful? What's wrong with me that my child isn't doing well in school? What am I doing wrong?"

A man, on the other hand, looks outward for the answer to problems in his life. "What's wrong here?" he'll ask. "What happened? Why didn't this work like I planned? What the heck happened?" He looks first to find the source of the problem in the *situation*, not in himself.

These are generalizations, of course, but they are pretty typical of male/female differences in how we respond to life events. A woman with a problem feels inadequate within herself, while a man with a problem feels frustrated by events or other people.

Is it any wonder, then, that we women sometimes feel that we're the only one with a problem we're having? We experience self-doubt about being good mothers to our kids; we feel inadequate to balance both work and family; we berate ourselves for what we think are "dumb mistakes." We are often our own worst critics—and to compound that harsh self-judgment, we keep our feelings to ourselves because we somehow think that we're the only one who ever felt this way! It's a vicious cycle, to be sure.

The first step in soothing and reassuring ourselves that we're NOT alone in our feelings of incompetence is to share our experiences—our stories—with other women. For it is in this sharing that we discover that we're not alone…and we're not all that incompetent!

"Life's challenges are not supposed to paralyze you;
they're supposed to help you discover who you are."

Bernice Johnson Reagon

PASS *the* SALT, PASS *the* GUILT

by Lisa Hammond

AS I SAT at the luncheon table, surrounded by a handful of successful women, I was amazed at how diverse the group was—an accomplished accountant, a technology expert, retail queen, a Pilates powerhouse, and more. Most of us ran our own businesses; most had children. We had gathered together for lunch—a rare bit of respite for such multitasking mavens!

In the midst of the salads and Diet Cokes, there was lots of laughter, plenty of groaning, and even a few tears. The thing that struck me the most was the fact that these accomplished— even award-winning women—all shared one thing in common: we felt like we were secretly deficient in some important way. Despite outward appearances, we felt we were somehow failing—failing at work because part of our brains wanted to be somewhere else; failing at being good mothers; failing at being the kind of dedicated wives we wanted to be; even failing our friends. Bottom line: we felt we were failing at the task of managing our overflowing lives.

Kelly, a mother of four, and a business owner, shared how painful it was to feel inadequate, never good enough, never having enough time, always shortchanging herself. Kelly also wondered aloud why men were not only missing the multi-tasking gene, but seemed unable to learn this vital skill. "Why didn't anyone warn me that girls and boys are so different?" she asked with more than a hint of exasperation.

Feeling inadequate or incompetent is not reserved just for mothers who work outside the home. During my own tour of duty as a stay-at-home mom, I felt completely useless at times. Ironically, it is the most important job I have ever done, and yet I felt unskilled, ineffective and unappreciated on most days.

Everyone at our lunch table roared with laughter when Shelly told us that she called a girlfriend so frequently for emotional support, she affectionately referred to her as "1-800-stay-at-home-friend." Shelly said she would call daily and ask to be reminded, "Tell me again, why is it that I'm staying home and why I thought this was a good idea?" Finally, Shelly had to get honest with herself and admit that she didn't enjoy being a stay-at-home mom. She started her own business and went back to work, only to discover that it came with its own set of challenges and judgments. Shelly summarized, "I wished someone had told me that not every woman is meant to be a stay-at-home mom, and that it's okay. It took me years to figure that out, and it was a very painful journey."

Just about the time our waiter came by to tempt us with the dessert tray, we were all starting to realize how common our worries, fears, and anxieties are. We are women—we are worrywarts!

"YOU NEED NOT FEEL GUILTY about not being able to keep your life perfectly balanced. Juggling everything is too difficult. All you really need to do is catch it before it hits the floor!"

Carol Bartz, president and CEO of Yahoo!

'Atta Girl

by BJ Gallagher

It's so easy for women
     to slip into self doubt
          and feeling inadequate.

After all,
we shoulder a lot of responsibilities—
     being supportive of our mates,
     nurturing our children,
     staying in touch with extended family,
     holding down jobs
     while holding down the fort at home.

No wonder we sometimes feel
     anxious,
          exhausted,
               insecure,
                    second-guessing ourselves.

We need to know
	we're not alone.
We need to hear
	that other women
share our experiences.

"'Atta girl" never sounded so sweet
	as when coming from the lips
		of another woman.
She understands,
	she's been there, done that.
She gets it—
	she gets *me.*

We take turns
	encouraging,
		supporting,
			cheering one another on.

We learn to do it for ourselves, too.
Just reach right over your shoulder, girl,
	and pat yourself on the back.

You're terrific,
	and you and I both know it.

LIVING IN THE SHADOW OF *Supermom*

by Tausha Seymour-Scarlett

MY MOM WAS MRS. COSBY. Just like on the Cosby TV show, my mother seemed perfect in every way: her domestic skills were superb; her household ran smoothly; she took care of sick or elderly relatives, in addition to caring for her own five children. She was a loving wife to my father AND she always had paying jobs outside the home as well! She was— and still is—phenomenal.

My mother (aka Lillian Elaine Seymour) has an amazing array of skills and talents. My father was in the Air Force, and every time our family moved, Mom would have the new place all squared away within 48 hours. Boxes would be unpacked, things put away, curtains hung, and everything in its place—she made it look effortless. Then she'd find herself a job, too—often in restaurant management. At one point she worked in a mortuary.

Later on in life, between her fourth and her fifth child (I was the fifth) Mom decided she wanted to be a nurse, so she went to nursing school and got her degree. I only remember her career in nursing, since I wasn't born when she had those other jobs. Not only was Mom a professional nurse, she took care of my father's mother when she was dying, and my grandmother as well. Mom was always taking care of everybody, it seemed—husband, kids, sick family members, even neighbors and friends.

It's wonderful to have such a competent, organized, loving mother when you're growing up, but I have to tell you, she's a hard act to follow. I have spent most of my adult life feeling bad about myself because I couldn't get it together like my mother always did. Clearly, I didn't inherit her "Domestic Goddess" gene. I try my best, year after year, but I just never can measure up to my Supermom.

Today, I have three kids of my own—ages 10, 7, and 2—as well as a husband and my own growing business. My house is tidy, my kids are well taken care of, and my husband is happy—but somehow, things are never perfect. I go to the pantry to make a peanut butter and jelly sandwich, only to discover that we're out of jelly. Or I invite a friend over for coffee and realize that I have no sugar in the house. It's little things like that—hundreds of them—that remind me that I'm falling short of my mother's standards.

And when she comes to visit—then it's really obvious. Just last week she called to discuss her trip plans and she said, "Can you make sure you have butter? Not that Country Crock stuff—I want real butter for my toast."

I think to myself, *Here we go . . .*

When I go to the market, I feel like a kid and think to myself: *I better not forget what Mom wanted me to get. Because God forbid she should complain, "My grandson doesn't have real butter!"*

Mom doesn't mean to be critical—she doesn't bring these things up to make me feel bad. In her own way, she's just trying to take care of us. She's not mean about it, but there's always a reminder that I just don't seem to have my act together—ever.

Even when she's not around, I feel the same way about myself. Whenever we're out of something at home, or the clean clothes don't make it out of the laundry basket into the drawers,

It's my fault.

In the past six months or so, I've started to make some progress in terms of feeling better about myself. I'm coming to accept the fact that I am not my mother—I am not Mrs. Cosby—I am not Florence Nightingale. I'm just me. But I know I still have a long way to go to come out of my mother's formidable shadow. It's probably a never-ending process.

The phrase "working mother" is redundant.

Jane Sellman, author, university professor

" It's not easy
being a mother.
If it were easy,
fathers would do it. "

Dorothy, a character on "The Golden Girls" TV show

We Feel Unworthy.

CHAPTER 2

FEELINGS OF UNWORTHINESS show up in a variety of ways—perhaps most clearly in our day-to-day conversations. Someone pays us a compliment and we shrug it off, "This old outfit? It's nothing special." Someone praises us and we resist the praise, saying, "Oh, it wasn't really a big deal." Or we try to pass the praise off to someone else, "I couldn't have done it without the help of others—they deserve most the credit." We sprinkle disclaimers throughout our conversations, betraying our lack of self-confidence: "It's just my opinion, but ..." or "This might be a silly idea ..." or "Maybe I'm wrong here, but ...." or "Maybe it's just me, but ..." or "I might be crazy, but ..." Most of us are not even conscious of how we betray our feelings of self-doubt and insecurity in our speaking.

There are other ways that unworthiness shows itself—with self-talk in our heads, in our feelings of being "less than" when we're with other people, and in our deference to those we deem smarter, more qualified, more successful and wealthier than we are. We play the comparison game all the time, to our own detriment.

Where do these feelings of "not enough" come from? There are a variety of influences on our self-image—early childhood experiences, our parents and siblings, teachers and preachers, TV and other media, and interactions with friends and community. Many of us had parents who meant well, but whose lack of skills or empathy, whose emotional deformities and/or demons, kept them from being the loving, supportive, caretakers that children need. No one sets out to be a bad parent, but some do a dismal job nonetheless.

Self-esteem problems are the most common result of negative programming in childhood. Little girls who are criticized, shamed, nagged, harassed and neglected—especially by their fathers and mothers—are highly likely to grow up with low or erratic self-esteem. Teachers, preachers and other authority figures can do a lot of damage, too—often under the guise of, "I'm doing this for your own good," or "You'll thank me someday."

Social messages received at school, in movies and television, in magazines and advertising, and in music and their accompanying videos, all convey messages about what it means to be a girl. The result of this non-stop bombardment of images and ideas is often not good. A girl who feels unattractive and/or unaccepted as a kid will almost always grow into a woman who doesn't feel good about herself. It shows up in myriad ways—insecurity, anxiety, poor posture, eating disorders, lack of self confidence, attraction to men who will continue to put her down or abuse her, and more.

Women who feel unworthy will often find ways to sabotage their own success at work, in romantic relationships and with money. Women who don't feel good about themselves have a difficult time accepting good fortune, success and love when it comes their way.

There are myriad ways in which unworthiness shows up in our lives. And in the end, it doesn't really matter how we got this way—the only thing that matters is what we do about it.

"Childhood is the first, inescapable
political situation each of us has to negotiate.
You are powerless.
You are on the wrong side in every respect.
Besides that, there's the size thing."

June Jordan, poet, essayist, activist

"Creative minds have always been known
to survive any kind of bad training."

Anna Freud, Austrian-born founder of child psychoanalysis,
daughter of Sigmund Freud

Sharp Words *Leave* Lasting Scars.

by BJ Gallagher

"WHAT'S THE MATTER WITH YOU? Can't you do anything right?" my father snapped at me as we walked up the steps to the courthouse. I had stumbled, almost falling. I was 16 at the time, and we had to go to court because I had been at fault in a fender bender. He was angry with me, understandably. But it felt like more than anger. It was a deep, intense resentment about my behavior reflecting badly on him.

I can still feel the white-hot harshness of his words. I didn't need a judge to pronounce me guilty—my father had already done it. His words felt like bullets from a verbal firing squad.

My spirit died a little that morning on the courthouse steps— one of many little "deaths" I experienced while growing up.

About ten years later, I was having a conversation with Dr. Roger Gould, a professor at UCLA. He told me he was working on a new book titled, *Recovering from Childhood*.

"That's the story of my life!" I exclaimed.

"It's the story of everyone's life," he replied. "Our parents spent the first 18 years raising us, then we spend the rest of our lives trying to undo the damage."

I found comfort in his words. For the first time in my life, I realized it wasn't just me.

It's been many years since that pivotal conversation with Dr. Gould. The process of re-programming "old tapes" has been long and challenging—but definitely worth it. And I've come to believe that all parents wound their children in one way or another—despite their best intentions. I'm a mother myself, and the last thing I ever wanted to do was hurt my child—but I know I did, in ways I didn't even realize.

Our parents did the best they could with who they were at the time, and we do the same with our own kids. We are all deeply flawed human beings, imperfect in oh-so-many ways. The best we can do is set about the business of healing our old childhood wounds, building a new stronger sense of self-worth, and encouraging others who are doing the same.

As my mother once said to me, "Blame your parents for the way you are; blame yourself if you stay that way."

"Self-esteem isn't everything;
it's just that there's nothing without it."

Gloria Steinem, feminist writer

ENOUGH

by BJ Gallagher

It's a familiar tune
running through my head ...

"Not pretty enough."
      "Not talented enough."
            "Not thin enough."
                  "Not smart enough."

The chorus sings,
      "Not enough! Not enough! Not enough!"

They're an a cappella group—
      the voices of Insecurity,
            Unworthiness,
                  and Self-doubt—
warbling their anxious refrain.

Sometimes Self-hatred joins in
      for a downbeat jam session.

I'm tired of their same old tune—
      "Not enough" on an endless loop.

How can I muffle their voices?
      Or get them to sing a new tune?

Oh, there they go again—
      do you hear them, too?

"Not enough,
      not enough,
            not enough ..."

Please, enough already!

The MESSENGER

is the MESSAGE.

by Nicki Keohohou

I WAS AT A SALES CONFERENCE in Australia recently
—it was a group of women in the direct sales business, provid-
ing cosmetics and beauty products to other women. One of the
things that struck me about these Australian women is that they
suffer from the "tall poppy syndrome." That is, if one woman
(poppy) starts to stand out in her field, people feel compelled to
cut her down. Or worse, she feels she must cut herself down.
This cultural belief makes it challenging for women to excel
and really let their lights shine.

One afternoon at the conference, a woman timidly raised her
hand in the middle of a workshop I was teaching. "If you have
a question," I reassured her, "there are probably 50 other
women here who have the same question. So by all means, ask
me anything."

She replied, "I feel like a fraud. I'm in the beauty business,
but I'm not beautiful. How can I ever be successful?"

I could feel the expectancy in the air as the group waited for
my answer. "How can you say you're not beautiful?" I asked
rhetorically. "Beauty comes in many colors, shapes, sizes and
contours. Some of the most beautiful women I know are not

beauty queens—but they have magnetic beauty nonetheless. Think of Maya Angelou. Think of Oprah. Think of the late Mother Teresa. Think of the late Golda Meir. Their inner beauty illuminated their features, making them glow from the inside out."

The next night their awards banquet was held, honoring the top saleswomen in the country. The woman who won the top three awards was what people would refer to as a "Plain Jane" —she had ordinary features, nothing striking or unique. But she had an energy about her, a sense of purpose and commitment, and above all, a belief in herself. As she collected award after award, I could hear the other women start to whisper among themselves, then they jumped to their feet applauding wildly. Several of them looked back at me, seated at a table behind them—they had tears in their eyes. They were witnessing what I had just told them the day before.

Beauty is as beauty does. Beauty is as beauty believes she is. Our "Plain Jane" award winner reassured the entire group that they are NOT frauds—they are NOT tall poppies that should be cut down—they are INDEED beautiful enough to be successful selling cosmetics. Most of all, they saw that they were not alone in feeling like they weren't "enough"—and they saw that their fear was unfounded.

"Your chances of success in any undertaking
can always be measured by your belief in yourself."

Robert Collier, motivational author

"I have a lot of things to prove to myself –
one is that I can live fearlessly."

Oprah Winfrey, media entrepreneur

We Fear
We Might
Be Crazy.

"AM I NUTS?" is a question that flits through the minds of most women sooner or later. Most of us have worried, at one time or another, that we're just a little bit crazy—or worse, that we've gone completely around the bend.

Psychologists report that men and women suffer many of the same kinds of emotional and mental health problems, but that women often LOOK crazier than men. Perhaps it's because we're more emotional than men—and more verbal—so our stress and distress are more visible to the world. Men often withdraw into themselves when they're distraught, but women do just the opposite—we cry, become hysterical and act out our anxiety in myriad ways.

Others around us may encourage us to "get a grip" or "snap out of it"—making us feel even more crazy and out of control. Whatever distress we're feeling is compounded by the fact that others criticize and judge us for our feelings. And we secretly worry that perhaps they're right—we fret that we're the only ones who are freaked out or strung out. We fear we're "going crazy."

In addition, some women have intense spiritual experiences; others feel the strong pull of intuition or psychic guidance; and still others encounter paranormal phenomena. Countless women never tell a soul, for fear of being seen as "crazy." Women have good reason to be circumspect in these matters, for history is replete with horrific punishments meted out by a society quick to condemn spiritually-gifted women as witches, or worse.

Today, we don't burn witches anymore, but we do ostracize, criticize and fear women we don't understand—women who appear "crazy." Is it any wonder then, that women who experience anything that smacks the least bit of the mystical, psychic or paranormal—or even just highly emotional—feel quite alone in their own realities? They worry that maybe society is right—perhaps they ARE crazy.

Fortunately, we live in a day and age where acceptance of all things psychic, metaphysical, and/or spiritual is growing. Mystics, gurus, shamans and priestesses are even respected and revered in some quarters—tolerated by others—and feared by only a small, but still vocal, minority.

Nonetheless, there are plenty of women who—for a variety of reasons—keep their secret worries about their own sanity to themselves. To them we would say, "Read on—find reassurance in the stories of women on the following pages—and take heart in the fact that you're probably not crazy, and you're certainly not alone."

"Those who can't hear the music
think the dancer quite mad."

anonymous

"*Some people march to the beat of a different drum*
. . . and some people polka."

Did you ever feel like a "*Crazy Mom*"...?

by BJ Gallagher

WHEN MY SON MICHAEL was 7 years old, I took him for weekly visits to his "temper doctor." Michael had been getting into trouble at school and after months of frustration, despair, and feeling like a failure as a mother, I finally took him to see a child psychologist.

Michael was a very sensitive boy, a musician and artist, and when other kids hurt his feelings or accidentally bumped into him or knocked his pencil off his desk, Michael always took it personally. He had a little touch of paranoia that made him suspect that these weren't just "accidents." Then he would overreact and punch the kid who had offended him. Needless to say, knocking another kid's block off did not sit well with teachers, nor the other kids. Michael spent many an hour in the principal's office and I received many a phone call from unhappy school officials telling me that Michael had decked another kid— again. Something had to be done about his temper.

After spending some time with Michael, the shrink gave me his diagnosis: "First, let me say that if this is the worst problem you have with your son, consider yourself lucky. I see far worse problems with many of the kids who are my clients."

Whew! That made me feel better right off the bat. My kid

was not some kind of violent brat. We were in the right place to get some help.

As the weeks turned into months, I saw the temper doctor a few times myself. Michael went to therapy once a week, and once a month I went along, too, for family therapy. A couple times I went without Michael for some extra parent coaching.

I recall one day I was particularly frustrated with the burden of being a single mom—it was so hard to make a living, raise my son, and still try to have some time for a social life. "Some days I get so angry and resentful that I just want to throw my kid out the window," I tearfully confessed. "Then I feel guilty and horrible—what kind of mom wants to throw her kid out the window? I hate myself. Am I going crazy?"

The doctor handed me a box of tissues as he reassured me, "Everything you're describing is normal. Almost all parents feel resentful sometimes. Kids change your life in ways you never anticipated. Parenthood is hard, and being a single mom is especially hard." He smiled in a kind, understanding way as he concluded, "It's OK to want to throw your kid out the window. It's not OK to actually DO it, but it's OK to want to do it. It's normal."

"Ohthankgod"… A huge burden of guilt and self-hatred was lifted from me, simply by sharing my deep, dark awful secret with someone who not only understood—but told me it was common. I wasn't alone in having moments of resentment toward my child. I wasn't the only mom who ever felt like this.

Sharing that secret with the shrink—and being reassured that I was not crazy—made it possible for me to share my experience with other mothers over the years. And without exception, they too, felt enormous relief to learn that negative feelings do not mean you're a crazy mother.

It's been 30 years since that conversation with the "temper doctor" and I am happy to tell you that I never did throw my kid out the window. I am also happy to tell you that those times of frustration and anger came fewer and farther between, as Michael and I both matured and learned how to handle our feelings.

But I must confess that on occasion—although very rarely—I can still get so frustrated I want to throw him out a window. But then I have to wonder, *Are there days when he wants to throw me out a window, too?*

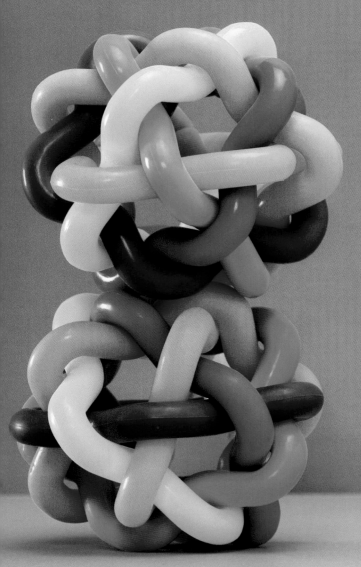

" Insanity is hereditary. You can get it from your children. "

Sam Levenson, author and humorist

"Mothers are all slightly insane."

J.D. Salinger, novelist, short story writer

THE *Mind* IS A DANGEROUS PLACE ... DON'T GO IN THERE ALONE.

by BJ Gallagher

The shrinks all say,
"If you think you're insane,
        you're not.
Crazy people don't know
        they're crazy."

I hope the shrinks are right,
        but sometimes I wonder ...

On those days
when every last nerve is frayed—
        I swear,
                if someone looks at me funny,
                I'll lose it.

Or those times
when I'm wracked with insecurity and doubt—
        I just can't handle
                one more thing going wrong.

Am I the only one
        who fears she's losing her marbles?

Am I merely "high strung"—
     or a full-blown neurotic?

Am I just "charmingly eccentric"—
     or genuinely certifiable?

Am I simply overwrought and overwhelmed—
     or suffering a nervous breakdown?

How can I tell
if I'm having a spiritual experience—
     or a delusional one?

Experts say
there's a fine line
between genius and madness,
     and I worry . . .
               because I was always the girl
               who colored outside the lines.

I'm driving myself crazy,
     wondering if I'm crazy!

My carpenter friend reassures me:
     "Nah, you're just half a bubble off plumb."
That makes me smile
     and relax a little.

No straight jacket for me—
     at least not today.

"If we weren't all crazy, we'd just go insane."

Jimmy Buffett. singer, songwriter

"The world thinks

eccentricity in great things is genius,

but in small things, only crazy."

Edward G. Bulwer-Lytton, British poet and novelist

AM *I* MY SISTER'S *Keeper*...OR IS *she* MINE?

by Lisa Hammond

MY SISTER has given me a lot of great gifts over the years, but the thing I treasure most is her honesty. Her bravery in sharing her journeys—both light and dark—is an inspiration to me. She has gone through crushing depression more than once and always comes out the other side. She has felt crazy and she's *been* crazy. Some university should award an honorary pharmaceutical degree to her for all the work she's done in trying to balance the chemicals in her brain. She is an amazing woman with vast amounts of courage and a wicked sense of humor.

My beloved and funny sister has actually lived through the thing many women fear (or have been threatened with)—men in white jackets coming to haul us away to a padded cell and/or a lithium drip. Well, they did haul away my sister, but today she can laugh about it. And today, whenever I feel crazy, she reminds me about the time it actually happened to her—and we share a chuckle.

Over the years, I have often called my dear sister, my life-line, when I felt like I was crossing the line between sane and crazy—when I thought my own nervous breakdown was imminent. Every time I reach out to her, she reminds me—over and over again—that I can check into a five-star hotel, order room service and get a massage every day for a week for a lot less money than what it costs to check into a sanitarium. She should know! She is still trying to pay off her medical bills from her last stay in the psych ward and she says she would have been better off at a resort. She jokes that all she got was bad hospital food, scratchy sheets and poor counseling.

So whenever I feel like I am clinging to my last shred of sanity, I call my lifeline—she reminds me there is a reason so many women feel like they are about to have a nervous breakdown: they need a break. And she gives me permission to take one.

" TO THE ANCIENT Chinese curse, 'May you live in interesting times,' we can add the feminist hex, 'May you live with unlimited options,' and when they present themselves, just say 'yes.' Losing your mind is a small price to pay for an interesting life."

Wendy Reid Crisp, author, magazine editor

We Fear We're
Unlovable.

ONE OF THE MOST memorable moments in the history of the Academy Awards was in 1984, when Sally Field stood at the podium—face beaming, clutching her Best Actress Oscar to her bosom—and blurting out, "You like me ... *you really like me!*" There wasn't a woman watching the awards that night who didn't know what Sally meant. We laughed because we all knew exactly how she felt.

Another famous actress, Marilyn Monroe, years earlier expressed similar feelings when she said, "I am not interested in money. I just want to be wonderful." Her words were different but her message the same, "I just want you to love me."

The need for love is not confined to actresses—all women feel it. The longing to be loved is universal. The thing we all want most in life is love—in whatever form is most meaningful to us.

For some women, love means having an adoring boyfriend or husband; for others love means having lots of good friends; for some, love takes the form of professional recognition and

fame. For many women, a loving family is what we want. And for others, money and gifts are proof of love. The form love takes varies from woman to woman, but the need for love is something we all share.

But having love in your life is no guarantee that you *feel* it or *recognize* it. Many women struggle with feelings of being unlovable, despite ample evidence to the contrary. These women cannot let love in because they harbor a deep-seated fear that they're not worthy.

Some go to great lengths to try to win more and more love and approval, driven by a haunting fear that if anyone ever really got to know them, they would discover a horrible secret—they're unlovable. One woman described it like Joseph Conrad's *Heart of Darkness*: *"I just know that if anyone ever got close enough to me to see into my heart, they would run away screaming, 'The horror, the horror!' I have this sense that although people think I am sweet and nice—at my core something is rotten. I fear that no one **really** loves me."*

When pressed, she acknowledged, *"I guess the real truth is that I don't love myself. So how can I believe that anyone else loves me? If I believe that I'm inherently unlovable, then being loved by others is—by definition—impossible."*

Sharing these fears about our lovability is a powerful way to begin to dissolve and dissipate the fear. When Sally Field shared her insecurity with the world that night, wasn't she met with an outpouring of empathy and understanding? You bet. So, when we share our deepest anxiety about our lovability, aren't we likely to discover the same thing that Sally discovered? People like us ... *they really like us!*

"One is taught by experience to put a premium on those few people who can appreciate you for what you are."

Gail Godwin, novelist

I WISH I'D *Danced.*

by Diane Boynton

wall-flow-er:

{1} a person who, because of shyness, unpopularity or lack of a partner, remains at the side at a dance or a party.

Sure, Cinderella's step-sisters were mean—no one wanted to take them to the ball. They were probably perfectly nice young ladies who turned bitter and angry after being left out.

Some say that, "everything in life happens for a reason." But with my high school years long behind me—and my family, for all intents and purposes, up and raised—I still don't see any "blessing" in being a high school wallflower. I've known success since then and I've overcome obstacles, but through it all, I still wish I'd been asked to a dance. Surely, I can't be the only one?

I wasn't unpopular and didn't experience the horrors of bullying that you hear about today. I struggled with my weight and there were not as many overweight teens as there are today,

so being a larger-size girl was lonely. But I was smart and good grades came easily; I enjoyed school. For the most part, I was liked by teachers and class-mates. I had great friends at church and school—we laughed together through many great experiences. In retrospect, my life could have been much worse.

But there is still one thing that can strike dread in the heart of a young woman—being the girl that no boy wants to date or dance with. Many a "smart girl" would happily trade good grades, a friend or two, and a smart brain to be the object of a young man's desire.

I'm sure the experience of the teenage boy has its own angst but I can only share the experience of a teenage girl who never dated and was never asked to a dance. It colored my perception of myself and my value to the world for many years.

If I could spend some time now with the girl I was then, the one who felt so left out and unloved, I would reassure her that brighter days are ahead. High school doesn't last forever and an entire world of possibilities is still up ahead. Dating will come later and love will show up, too—it does for almost everybody.

In recent years, I've learned that singles and groups of friends are now going to proms. That wasn't happening when I was a teenager. If you didn't have a date, you stayed home. Times have changed and it warms my heart every time I see youth of all shapes, sizes and ethnicities out having a good time. Nothing can be more important than having a strong sense of self, but there has to be an easier way to learn your own value, without feeling unwanted and left out.

I'd encourage anyone who has a son or daughter missing out on an important rite of passage or common youthful experience to do whatever you can to help these young people find a way to dance.

"It is not easy to find happiness in ourselves, and it is not possible to find it elsewhere."

Agnes Repplier, essayist, social critic

MONEY AND *Love*

by BJ Gallagher

MY STEP-MOTHER Christine and I had had a lovely afternoon, one of those "girls' day out" kind of things. We had lunch at a wonderful cafe, visited some charming boutiques in the desert resort where she and Dad live, and finished our afternoon off with a movie. We had a great time. I often think Christine is more like my sister rather than my step-mom. We have similar tastes, interests and outgoing personalities—and because she is 20 years younger than Dad, she is closer to my age than to his. We have become good friends and confidantes over the years.

We drove back to the condo where she and Dad have lived since they retired. As we got out of the car, Christine took several of her packages from the back seat and put them in the trunk. She had just one small shopping bag in her hand, which she was going to take into the house. As I got out of the car, I said, "I think I'll put my purchases in my car, so I don't have to take them into the house and then into the car later. I'll save myself some work." But what I really meant was, "I'm going to put my bags in my car so Dad won't see them. I don't want him to know I spent any money." Christine and I were both on the same wavelength—and we knew it.

Dad is from the Great Depression generation, and he has always been frugal. I tease him, "Dad, they don't have luggage racks on hearses, you know!" He laughs and replies, "If I can't take it with me, I'm not going!"

His thriftiness is both a virtue and a vice. The positive side is that he always has money in savings for emergencies and he doesn't lose sleep over debt. All his bills and taxes get paid on time and he feels secure that he won't outlive his savings. The negative side of frugality is that he worries about not getting the best possible deal. He hesitates on investments too long, is fearful of losing money and then misses the opportunity entirely. His children sometimes think that he doesn't love them when he won't buy something they want.

Is my Dad the only man in the world like this? Are Christine and I the only two women who hide purchases from the men in their lives?

What's the story here?

It's taken me years to "come out of the closet" where money is concerned. Money is the last taboo in our society—people will talk about their sex lives, their dysfunctional families, alcohol and drug problems, abusive relationships, their illnesses and bodies, their struggles with God—but discussion of money is still verboten. Money is just way too intimate and personal—but the secrecy often leads to feelings of shame, guilt and confusion.

Money is tricky stuff—intertwined with issues of power and control, ego and status, self-esteem and respect. Many of us make an emotional connection between money and love—I know that I did. My Dad is tight with money and tight with his time, attention and approval. My Mom is generous with herself and her money, deriving enormous pleasure in giving to others. Of course I would grow up equating money with love! Am I the only one? Somehow I don't think so.

How women and men handle their money speaks volumes about their families, whether or not they feel loved, how they provide for their children, and how they deal with issues of control, power, sex and loyalty. Hiding purchases is just one small example of how our emotional issues are reflected in our financial behavior.

Isn't it time we bring money out of the closet, open up the family checkbook, and commit to some financial healing with one another?

"From birth to age 18,
a girl needs good parents; from 18 to 35
she needs good looks; from 35 to 55 she needs
a good personality; and from 55 on
she needs cash."

Sophie Tucker, vaudeville entertainer

MY BODY, *Myself*

by Barbara Jensen

SEVERAL YEARS AGO I attended a women's seminar, "Understanding Men," which included a panel of men to answer our questions. We spent the afternoon listening to men tell us how they think and feel.

The question I asked was, "How important is a woman's weight in terms of her attractiveness to men?" The oldest of the four men took the lead. He was a stocky guy with a full head of hair, great smile and exuding an air of relaxed confidence. He looked out over the group of women and said, "Well, ladies, how important is a *man's* weight to his attractiveness?" He laughed, then continued: "Let me tell you, it's not about weight at all. A woman who feels good about herself is really sexy to men—you can tell how a woman carries herself, her grooming, how she dresses and acts. *A woman who loves herself is attractive to men*—it has nothing to do with weight." The other three men concurred.

I was both relieved and challenged. I realized that my life-long obsession with weight and appearance had more to do with my relationship with myself than with men. I discovered that my problem wasn't about whether guys loved me—*it was about whether I loved me.*

I don't know about you, but nowhere does this self-love challenge show up more than in relationship with my body. It started very young: I was 12 years old, 5'8" tall, and weighed only 120 pounds, but I *felt* like an Amazon—too tall, too big, too fat. Those were painful years.

Today, I look back and see that my whole life I've had a "fat head"—no matter how little I weighed, I always thought I was fat . . . and that meant I was unlovable.

Can we ever set ourselves free from our obsession with body image? Can we find a way to accept ourselves—*to love ourselves?* There is at least some comfort in knowing that we're not alone in our anxiety about sexiness and attractive-ness. Millions of women share this insecurity. When it comes to body image and feeling good about ourselves, we still have a long way to go, baby.

THE

Unanswerable
QUESTION

by BJ Gallagher

Do you love me?
    Yes.

Do you really love me?
    I said yes.

No, I mean,
do you really, really love me?
    Yes, I love you.

How about now?
Do you love me now?
    Yes, I love you now.

And now?
Do you still love me?
> *How many times*
> *do I have to tell you?*
> *… I love you.*

Show me you love me.
> *No matter how much I love you,*
> *it will never be enough.*

Don't be silly.
I was just asking a simple question.
> *I think the real question is—*
> *Do YOU love you?*

Don't change the subject.
I still need to know if you love me . . .

"You yourself,
as much as anybody
in the entire universe,
deserve your love
and affection."

Buddha

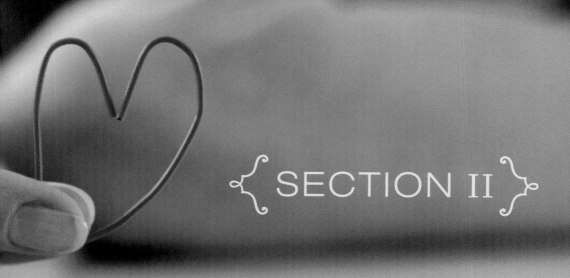

{ SECTION II }

SEVEN WONDERFUL
WAYS OF CONNECTING
AND SHARING.

READING STORIES about other women's struggles and feelings of unworthiness, insecurity and self-doubt can help you see your own worries and fears more clearly. The power in sharing our stories is learning that we aren't alone.

We invite you to think about what you learned from the stories— are there ideas and lessons that you can apply in your own life? We offer the following seven tips as a good starting point:

{1}   Give Up the Need To Be Perfect.

{2}   Open Up and Share Your Feelings.

{3}   Forgive Yourself . . . and Others, Too.

{4}   Ask for Help.

{5}   Rebound and Reinvent.

{6}   Choose Friends Worth Having.

{7}   Go Where the Love Is.

After all, you have nothing to lose but your fear, anxiety, worry, self-doubt and loneliness.

Let the sharing begin!

Give Up the Need
to be Perfect.

CHAPTER 1

"The thing that is really hard,
and really amazing, is giving up on being perfect and
beginning the work of becoming yourself."

Anna Quindlen, journalist, author

"In nature, nothing is perfect and everything is perfect.
Trees can be contorted, bent in weird ways,
and they're still beautiful."

~ Alice Walker, author

Martha Stewart

...NOT!

by Lisa Hammond

IT WAS OCTOBER, so it was time for me to start talking about having a Halloween party—something I have done for at least half a dozen years. I don't actually end up having a Halloween party; I just talk about having one. It has become a running joke around our house.

Entertaining and having friends over for dinner always seems like such a good idea but the truth is, I just never feel like I am good enough to actually do it.

I have ongoing chatter in my head that goes something like this: *What are you going to make? Who are you going to invite? You don't have the time. You will say you are going to do this and then you won't get out of the office in time.*

I have plenty of friends who seem to be able to manage both a successful career and entertaining frequently. They race home from work, whip up three-course meals and serve the perfect wine. They look calm, cool and collected when guests arrive. I am both impressed—and depressed—by this.

Recently, I wanted to be a thoughtful dinner guest at a friend's home so I decided to at least bring dessert. Although I had a jam-packed day at work, I didn't want to be a slacker, and figured I could handle making a cake. I did what I have done countless times—I decided to make a favorite family recipe, Raspberry Cream Cake.

Once I started to make the cake, I remembered why I don't do it very often—half of the ingredients can only be found in the state where the recipe came from! So I had to wing it and substitute ingredients. Then the mixer fell apart as I was using it and whipped cream went flying all over the kitchen. Then the cake burned while I was stuck on a conference call. When I finally got the cake into the fridge for the mandatory five hours of chilling prior to being served, I decided to rename it the Raspberry Curse Cake and vowed never to make it again.

When my husband and I arrived at the dinner party—crappy Curse Cake in hand, our gracious hostess was looking relaxed as she put together a simple salad. And there I was—frazzled, with raspberry juice still in my hair. As we sat down to dinner I asked her for the recipe for the delicious rice dish she was serving. She laughed and handed me her phone as she said, "Are you kidding me? I didn't have time to cook all of this—it's take-out!"

Oh, I have so much to learn from other women! I had been stressing out all day, trying to simultaneously work and bake a cake, juggling mixers and conference calls and cursing like a sailor—while my wise friend had been at work phoning in take-out!

The entire episode made me realize how much pressure women are under to be all and do all—almost all of it self-imposed! How much are we missing out on because of our insecurity and fear?

By the time you read this, I will have invited friends over for margaritas and dinner at our place—paper plates, take-out food and fun will be had by all!

"Ring the bells that still can ring.

Forget your perfect offering.

There is a crack, a crack in everything.

That's how the light gets in."

Leonard Cohen, Canadian poet, singer/songwriter

You are perfectly
IMPERFECT...

Individual and unique

Miraculous and surprising

Patient with your foibles

Emotionally honest

Ready to laugh at yourself

Free to fail sometimes

Embracing your own contradictions

Comfortable in your own skin

Tested and tempered by life

Open Up and Share Your Feelings.

CHAPTER 2

"Women best understand each other's language."

Teresa of Avila, Catholic nun, mystic, author

"It is the friends you can call up at 4 a.m. that matter."

~ Marlene Dietrich, German actress

TIME TO TAKE OFF *the Mask.*

by BJ Gallagher

I CRIED ALL THE WAY home from the party. The man that I was deeply in love with had been there ... with a date. I was devastated. He and I had broken up some months earlier and I was still grieving the end of our love affair. I knew that he would be at the party, since this was a celebration for faculty and graduate students in my department at the university, and he was a faculty member. So of course he would be there. But I thought he would come alone.

How could he show up with a date?

But I never let him, or anyone else, see my pain—in fact, just the opposite. I was at my charming best. I looked great, wearing a new outfit I had bought for the occasion. I was funny, entertaining, the life of the party. I regaled everyone with great stories and jokes, flirting at every chance, and putting on quite a show. I made sure that people had a great time.

Then the evening was over and I drove home, alone. Sobbing all the way, I felt hurt that no one comforted me in my pain. *Why didn't they see through my act?* I asked myself. *Why didn't someone take me aside and reassure me that it was going to be OK, that I was going to be OK?*

The next day I had lunch with my friend, Donna. My eyes were still red from the night of crying. I complained to her

about how unhappy I was that none of my friends at the party had supported me in the way I wanted them to.

"Why would they?" she asked me. "You were giving them all a great time. Why would they want you to stop?"

I was stumped.

"I don't know," I replied.

"Here's the deal," she explained. "You make life wonderful for your friends by always being 'on.' You put on your beautiful mask, you're charming and funny, and you've trained them to see you in this way. It's not their fault that you're putting on an act. It's your fault. You've done this to yourself. You can't blame them."

Well, she really had me there. She was right. I had created this delightful public persona that now I felt compelled to maintain, under all circumstances. What could I do?

"Why don't you try just being yourself," she suggested in that soft, gentle way of hers. "Try it a little bit at a time. See what happens."

What did I have to lose? Nothing but the burden of being constantly charming. So I tried it. The next time I was depressed, I just showed up the way I was. I watched to see if any of my friends turned away. Nope. They were still my friends. And they accepted me whether I showed up happy or sad. What an amazing discovery! Gradually, over time, I was willing to reveal more and more of what I was feeling. And still no one ran away from me. It took several years of slowly revealing more and more of who I really was, and what was going on with me, to come completely out of my emotional closet.

My friend Donna gave me a lovely gift—the gift of being myself. I don't know where I ever got the crazy idea that I had to be cheerful and charming all the time to keep my friends happy with me—it doesn't matter. All that matters is that I had a true friend who untied my mask so that I could take it off.

What a relief!

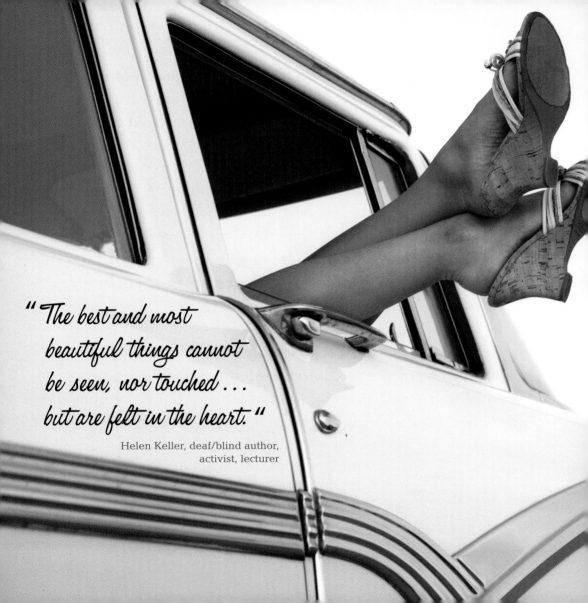

" The best and most
beautiful things cannot
be seen, nor touched . . .
but are felt in the heart. "

Helen Keller, deaf/blind author,
activist, lecturer

Wise women know how to LISTEN to one another:

Lean in to establish rapport.

Interpret feelings
   as well as words.
Stay connected through
   eye contact.
Tune in to what's not being said
   as well as what is.
Express empathy
   and understanding.
Never interrupt, criticize,
   or judge...just LISTEN.

Forgive Yourself
...and Others, Too.

CHAPTER 3

"Forgiveness is the key to action and freedom."

Hannah Arendt, philosopher

"Forgiveness is the act of admitting

we are like other people."

Christina Baldwin, author

Forgiveness

by Maya Angelou

I DON'T KNOW if I continue, even today, always liking myself. But what I learned to do many years ago was to forgive myself. It is very important for every human being to forgive herself or himself because if you live, you will make mistakes—it is inevitable. But once you do and you see the mistake, then you forgive yourself and say, "Well, if I'd known better I'd have done better." That's all.

So you say to people whom you think you may have injured, "I'm sorry," and then you say to yourself, "I'm sorry." If we all hold on to the mistake, we can't see our own glory in the mirror because we have the mistake between our faces and the mirror; we can't see what we're capable of being.

You can ask forgiveness of others, but in the end the real forgiveness is in one's own self. I think that young men and women are so caught by the way they see themselves. Now mind you, when a larger society sees them as unattractive, as threats, as too black or too white or too poor or too fat or too thin or too sexual or too asexual, that's rough. But you can overcome that.

The real difficulty is to overcome how you think about yourself. If we don't have that we never grow, we never learn, and sure as heck we should never teach.

"How life catches up with us and teaches us
to love and forgive each other."

Judy Collins, singer

How do you find
FORGIVENESS?

Feel your hurt.

Open your mind.

Release your anger.

Give love a chance.

Inquire within your heart.

Venture into dialogue.

Embrace the other person.

Nudge yourself to keep at it,
even when you don't want to.

Enjoy new possibilities and freedom.

Seek Divine guidance and help.

Savor your new serenity and peace.

Ask for Help.

CHAPTER 4

"Three of the most powerful
words in the English language are
'Please help me.'"

Cathy Conheim, therapist, author

Learning to *Ask* for what we *Need.*

by Susan Belgard

DONNA WAS A GIVER, a caretaker, someone who was always going out of her way to help others. In her mid-40s, Donna was a remarkably generous person and I loved her dearly. She was my best friend. We lived near each other in San Francisco and often went to movies, parties, plays and other things together.

I started working several days a week in San Diego. One day I called Donna while I was away, and I could hear something different in her voice. She said simply, "I've been diagnosed with cancer." Those are words you never want to hear from your best friend . . . or from anyone, for that matter. I was in shock. Her next words would change my life forever, opening a new dimension of experience that I could never have anticipated. "I have to go to the doctor in a few days to get the results of my MRI, and I don't want to go alone. Would you go with me?" she asked.

Her request was nothing short of remarkable . . . and an enormous gift. It was the beginning of a process in which she taught me how to ask for help, how to receive with grace and dignity, and how to bring together the people who love you when you need them most. Donna knew that she wanted people around her—that no matter what the future held, she did not want to go through this alone. Over the next few months, I watched her as she gently organized her friends into a loose, but effective support system.

There were eight of us in the core group, and we had a meeting (without Donna present) to discuss what we could do and what we couldn't. We talked about how we felt about her illness—our own emotions and feelings. We made commitments in whatever way we could, to provide what Donna needed. In the beginning, she needed three primary things: to get to work, to get out to social activities, and to get to doctors' appointments. She also needed us to spread the word and tell her other friends, to save her from the emotional and physical drain of having to explain her illness again and again.

We took shifts helping Donna.

Since I was away for part of each week, I had the evening role, with a tuck-in call to her every night to see how she was doing as she went to bed. Others had morning duties, afternoon commitments, etc. So in our core group, we didn't see each other much, but we didn't need to. We were a virtual support team, like ships passing in the night, each of us committed to the same goal—to be there for Donna.

As time went on, her needs changed and grew. More people pitched in and helped out in various ways—cooking, cleaning, helping with medical care. In the final month of Donna's life, a relative of hers came to stay . . . and so did my cat. Donna had always loved my cat, and she asked if he could come and be with her. Of course, I said "yes." He was a sweet guy—I'm sure he didn't mind being loaned to my dying friend.

The fact that she could ask for what she needed and wanted continued to impress me. She made it so much easier for us. She recognized that good friends always want to help—but they often don't know how. It is such an awkward situation . . . your friend has six months to live and you don't know what to say or do. Sometimes people just disappear when their friends are ill or dying, because they can't handle their own awkwardness.

Donna solved that problem for us. She knew what she needed and she took the initiative to ask. What remarkable courage! What remarkable grace and poise!

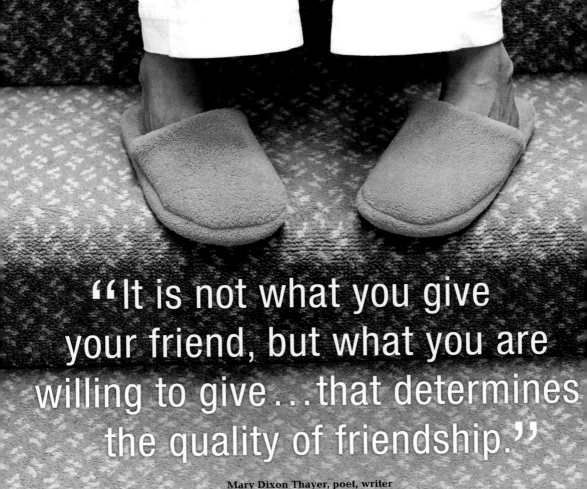

"It is not what you give your friend, but what you are willing to give...that determines the quality of friendship."

Mary Dixon Thayer, poet, writer

People find joy in GIVING...

Going the extra mile

Involved in each other's lives

Vested interest in mutual well-being

Inquiring how best to help

Needing one another

Growing by giving

Rebound and Reinvent.

CHAPTER 5

"We don't know who we are

until we see what we can do."

Martha Grimes, author

The First Wife

by Arianna Arapakis

I FELT SO FOOLISH when my husband divorced me after 20 years. I had been the dutiful wife—always putting him first, looking good for him, entertaining his business associates, maintaining a beautiful home, raising our son. And when he replaced me with a younger woman, I wondered: *Am I the only woman who has been so foolish? I lost myself in our married life and suddenly I found myself out on my own—terrified, confused, betrayed and alone. Was I a complete fool?*

Tommy and I met when we were in our late twenties. He was crazy about me and very insistent that I was the girl for him. I wasn't so sure he was the guy for me. I didn't feel the chemistry with Tommy that I'd felt with other boyfriends.

After two years of dating, I agreed to marry him. I wasn't madly in love, but he seemed like good "husband material"—responsible, hard-working, ambitious, thoughtful, and the kind of guy who will take care of his wife and family. We settled into domestic life together.

I worked in my father's restaurant business until I had my son, Johnny. Then I was able to stay at home as a full-time mom, and was grateful that I could. After a couple years at home, I was ready for more adult conversation and went back to work again, part-time.

I was very supportive of Tommy and his business ambitions. He was the credit manager for a recycling company and there are a lot of political aspects to that business—securing city contracts, and stuff like that. So there was a lot of entertaining required to schmooze with clients. I had very few friends of my own—having neglected my girlfriends in favor of my husband's business associates.

Tommy began to travel a lot on business. Increasingly I felt that something was missing in our marriage—chemistry—and I longed for that.

I made the mistake of getting emotionally involved with another guy. Nothing physical ever happened, but we talked on the phone all the time. When Tommy found out, he went ballistic. He told me our marriage was over and yelled, "You have to move out!"

Ultimately, he calmed down and I didn't move out after all. We decided we both wanted to work on our marriage.

A few months later, a sympathy card arrived at our house, and it was very odd. It was sent anonymously to Tommy, but I opened it since we had agreed not to have secrets anymore. It said something like, "Now, what are you going to do for your 'action' on the side?" It referred to the fact that his secretary was getting married. I confronted Tommy about the note and he denied everything. He said it was just someone who didn't like him, playing a cruel joke. I believed him.

A year later, it was Tommy's turn to confront me. He told me that he wanted out. "Look, we never did have any chemistry," he said. And he was right. But it still came as a shock. I had done my very best to make a go of it with Tommy, and now, here I was, facing something I never thought I would have to deal with—divorce. I was terrified.

That was in early 2004—a very hard year. Our son left for college while I was trying to get my new catering business up and running; and my husband wanted a divorce. I moved out in late 2004. It was gut-wrenching. I lost my home, my husband, and even my dog Zeus. I lost my friends, too, because they were all Tommy's business friends. I was devastated.

To add insult to injury, Tommy's secretary divorced her husband and moved in with mine. It turns out that Tommy had been having an affair with his secretary long before he divorced me. And now she has everything that I spent 20 years building—my house, my social life, my vacation home, and yes, my dog. She just stepped right into my life.

I've had no contact with Tommy since then—it's been like a death. I'm sure that getting a divorce was the best thing for both of us, but even when you know it's for the best, it still hurts.

I've grown tremendously since 2004. I have my own friends and my own interests. I'm dating and I've rediscovered passion again—which is wonderful. Never again will I settle for a relationship without passion. I pay attention to my internal dialogue and trust my intuition. I'm much less interested in material things because I had all those things when I was married and they didn't make me happy. For the first time in my life, I am my own woman. It's still not easy and sometimes I cry when I think of the past. But I'm reinventing myself—bit by bit every day.

Here's how to
REBOUND...

Reevaluate your future.

Explore new options.

Bounce back quickly.

Overcome disappointment.

Uncover hidden strengths.

Never give up on yourself.

Develop wisdom and perspective.

"Holding onto a resentment is like swallowing poison and hoping the other person will die."

anonymous

Choose Friends
Worth Having.

CHAPTER 6

"Friends are the family we choose for ourselves."

Edna Buchanan, journalist and crime novelist

WEEDING *your* FRIENDSHIP GARDEN

by Cynthia Cameron

A FEW YEARS AGO, I went to a seminar called, "Be the CEO of Your Life" and took one of those personal assessments that help you see yourself more clearly. One of the statements we were asked to respond to was, "I have let go of relationships that harm me." It really struck home.

I had a longtime friend that I'd know since we were schoolgirls—her name is Maria. Over the years, Maria seemed to become more negative, cynical and caustic. She went through a divorce, had disappointments in her career, and her life just wasn't turning out like she had hoped. Her personality changed and the fun friendship we had when we were younger dissipated, leaving in its place someone I still loved but didn't like.

One afternoon, Maria and I were both at a BBQ at a mutual friend's home. A bunch of us were standing around talking and Maria mentioned that she was having a gathering at her house next month and asked if I would come. I said, "Oh, I can't. I have family coming that weekend, so I can't make it." She replied sarcastically, "You know, you don't have to make up a lie. If you don't want to come, just say so." Then she laughed. This conversation took place right in front of a bunch of our friends.

In that instant, something clicked in my head and I made a decision: *I'm done. I don't need this. I'm finished with her.*

It wasn't a big loss, really. We only saw each other a couple times a year and the only time she ever called was when she wanted something. By the time I made my decision, it wasn't much of a friendship anymore anyway.

Some months later, she called and left a message, asking me to help her spruce up her resume. I didn't return the call. A few weeks later, my friend, Keisha, asked me, "What's the deal with you and Maria? She said you didn't return her call. She's complaining to the rest of us."

I explained to Keisha that I didn't want to be friends with Maria anymore, and I told her why. "It's fine if you and the others want to be friends with her—doesn't bother me a bit. Just please don't include me in things where Maria's involved."

What was so interesting was that the other women were feeling the same way about Maria, but no one spoke up! It turns out that we were all just putting up with this toxic woman in our lives.

That was four years ago and I am still happy I made that decision. Today, I choose to select people who are positive, who have goals, who want to be successful—emphasis on the word choose. It doesn't matter how long I've known the friend—if her energy and attitude feels harmful, I walk away. It's shaped my choice of new friends, too. I only want positive people in my life.

Tending friendships is like gardening. Sometimes a plant that you thought was a flower turns out to be a weed—it has to be pulled out before it crowds out other flowers. Or, sometimes a plant dies and it has to be dug up and discarded. It's all part of maintaining a lovely garden that nourishes your spirit and refreshes your soul. You can't let the weeds and dead plants ruin your garden.

❝ EACH FRIEND REPRESENTS a world in us, a world possibly not born until they arrive, and it is only by this meeting that a new world is born."

Anais Nin, French-born diarist

What does it mean to be a
TRUE FRIEND?

Trust
Respect
Understanding
Empathy

Forgiveness
Responsiveness
Insight
Expressions of love
Needing one another
Dependability
Spiritual connection

CHAPTER 7

Go Where
the Love Is.

"The meeting of two personalities

is like the contact of two chemical substances:

if there is any reaction, both are transformed."

Carl Jung, Swiss psychiatrist

"I ALWAYS THOUGHT I was the only one who couldn't control what I put in my mouth," Jo Anne says. "I suspected that my 'food thermostat' was broken—you know, the thing inside that tells you when you're full. Other people seemed to know when to stop eating, but I didn't. I would eat long past satisfying my body's hunger. I just kept eating and eating—between meals, while preparing meals, in the car, in front of the TV, late at night, grazing almost non-stop. For years I didn't know what was wrong with me—and what made it worse was I thought I was the only one.

"But then I discovered 12-step programs and I discovered a whole world of women who had eating problems, too, and my life changed. I felt enormous relief in discovering that there are lots of women like me—it made me feel less crazy. And not only did these women share my problem—they had also found a solution. For the first time, I had hope.

"There are several programs that deal with food—Over-eaters Anonymous, Food Addicts Anonymous, Compulsive Eaters Anonymous (CEA-HOW), and others. They all apply spiritual principles to problems with food and help us discover the emotional/spiritual hunger that has been driving our unhealthy eating habits."

Jo Anne says she has a compulsive-addictive personality—describing herself as a "Lifeaholic", rather than a foodaholic, or a shopaholic, or some other kind of addict. "It's not food or drugs or alcohol that are the problems," she explains. "The problem is that I don't know how to deal with Life—that's why I call myself a Lifeaholic. Somehow I didn't learn some of those basic life skills as a kid, and I turned to food and other mood-altering substances or activities to help me deal with day-to-day stress. I'm very sensitive and it often feels like my nerves are on the *outside* of my skin, not the inside. I always want a little something to help take the edge off—a little ice cream, some chocolate, a glass of wine, a new pair of shoes—anything to help make me feel a little better when Life gets to be too much."

Her story about discovering her addictive personality is a story that many women can identify with.

It's a story of looking for love in all the wrong places. Millions of women reach for something outside themselves in an attempt to feel better. Some of us reach for chocolate; others reach for a bottle; some reach for a credit card and head off on a shopping binge. Some women seek reassurance in addictive relationships with the wrong men; others become workaholics to calm their self-doubt with over-achievement. Some women resort to compulsive dieting and exercise to keep their demons at bay; while others troop off to physicians to get prescriptions for the newest, trendy *drug du jour*. All of these women are essentially on the same quest. They—and *we*—are looking for a little something to make us feel better about ourselves, to feel lovable.

Jo Anne is among the growing number of women who have given up looking for love in all the wrong places. She explains:

"All along what I *really* wanted was love—a hug, a smile, a friend, a lover, someone to talk to, someone who really understood me. But I didn't know how to get love, so I reached for things I *did* know how to get—food, alcohol, pills and new clothes. They were accessible, legal, easy to get, and they worked, at least for a little while. The problem is they didn't work long enough. I'd have to get another "fix"— another man, another shopping trip, another half-gallon of ice cream, whatever. But over time, the things that used to make me feel better started to make me feel worse. Food was my best friend, but then it turned on me. I gained weight and hated myself. But I

couldn't stop. My compulsive behavior was out of control—I was possessed by a demon I didn't understand.

"It wasn't until I found my way to programs like Overeaters Anonymous and Debtors Anonymous that I finally found a solution. I found people who understood me and didn't judge me. I found hugs, smiles, listening ears, compassionate hearts. Best of all, I finally experienced the unconditional love I had been looking for.

"They said, 'Let us love you until you can learn to love your-self.' And over time, bit by bit, slowly I began to feel more lovable. With their patient listening, wise guidance, and deep compassion, I'm learning to love myself."

Jo Anne says that she occasionally finds herself tempted again to resort to sugar or shopping to make herself feel better. She says, "Sometimes I feel empty or anxious. I am torn between Godiva or God. And I must confess, sometimes I still choose Godiva. But other times I remember to pick up the phone and call a friend, or go for a walk, or read a spiritual book, or simply bow my head and pray. I'm a work in progress, and I still have much to learn about how to look for love in all the *right* places."

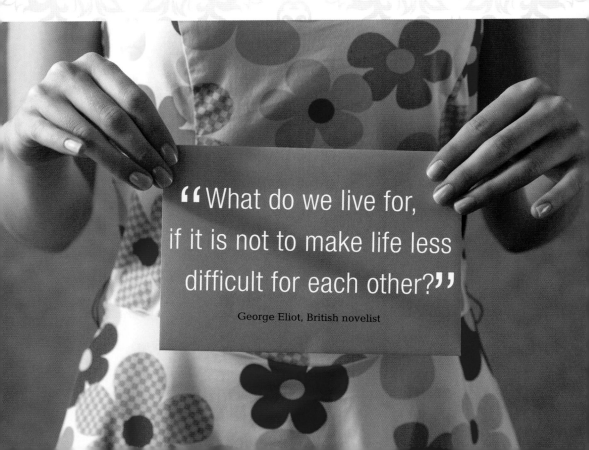

"*Love grows by giving. The love we give away is the only love we keep. The only way to retain love is to give it away.*"

Elbert Hubbard, philosopher, writer, publisher

"What do we live for, if it is not to make life less difficult for each other?"

George Eliot, British novelist

A friend who
LOVES you...

Laughs with you,
    not at you.

Opens her heart,
    her arms, and her home.

Voices her affection
    and appreciation.

Embraces you with
    unconditional acceptance.

Sees your talent and beauty,
    even when you don't.

Conclusion:
WOMEN *connecting* HEART *to* HEART

PSYCHIATRIST Scott Peck, author of *The Road Less Traveled*, gave a lecture years ago in which he said that the biblical phrase, "The kingdom of God is within you," was mistranslated. If you go back to the original Aramaic, in which the Bible was first written, what that phrase really says is, "The kingdom of God is *among* you." The kingdom of God is in community. "Wherever two or more are gathered, God is there."

Whether or not you believe in God, the idea that, "the whole is greater than the sum of its parts" is irrefutable. We are social creatures, meant to live in groups, clans, families, tribes, villages, neighborhoods, parishes—in partnership with others. When we come together and share who we are with one another, something magical happens. That's why support groups are so healing. It's why self-help programs are so successful—they tap into the power of community.

It is our deepest wish that you find connection and community in your own life. Take a chance and share your feelings, thoughts and experiences with other women who can validate the fact that you're not alone, you're not crazy, and there's nothing wrong with you.

Secrets can make us sick and holding our fears and anxieties inside can indeed make you feel like you're the only woman who ever felt like this. Too many of us have spent years worrying, *You're OK—I'm not OK*. Isn't it time to give that up?

As we end this book, we want to leave you with a final gift—your very own Declaration of Interdependence. Take it to heart; post it where you'll see it frequently; share it with others. Declare yourself FREE to be who you are—FREE to share who you are with the world.

DECLARATION *of* INTERDEPENDENCE

by BJ Gallagher *and* Lisa Hammond

We hold these truths to be self-evident:

That all women are created equal—
   but each is blessed with different gifts and talents.

That all women are endowed with certain individual rights—
   but each must assume shared responsibilities.

For the happiness of all
   depends on the commitment of each
      to support equality and individuality,
      rights and responsibilities.

We declare all women to be mutually interdependent—
   banding together to support one another,
   sharing our experience, strength, and hope,
      that all may enjoy life, love,
      and the pursuit of laughter.

We agree to encourage one another in tough times
   and celebrate in good times.

We commit to taking turns leading and following,
   inspiring and teaching,
      listening and learning.

We agree to give credit where credit is due—
   including us.

We commit to loving ourselves first—
   because we can't give what we don't have.

With this Declaration of Interdependence,
we set ourselves free—
   free from old beliefs that are no longer true,
   free from self-doubt, insecurity, and loneliness,
   free from self-imposed perfectionism.

We set ourselves free—
   heeding our intuition in all her guises,
   loving our bodies through every change,
   finding our voices to speak our own truths.

We set ourselves free—
   to create fulfilling work,
   to form nurturing families,
   and to build great friendships.

We are strong;
   we are beautiful;
      we are generous;
      we are wise.

We are women—
   committed to creating
   a world that affirms us all.

ABOUT *the* AUTHORS

LISA HAMMOND, known as The Barefoot CEO, founded Femail Creations, a mail order catalog and website with a unique selection of meaningful gifts by, for, and about women. Giving back is at the heart of Femail Creations—every issue of the catalog spotlights a charity making a difference in the lives of women and girls.

Lisa is the recipient of the SBA "Business Person of the Year Award," Moms In Business "Create Your Dreams Award," and the Soroptimist International Business & Organizations "Advancing the Status of Women Award."

Lisa's book *Dream Big: Finding the Courage to Follow Your Dreams and Laugh at Your Nightmares* (Conari Press; 2004) has become a best-seller. Her other books include: *Stepping Stones* (Red Wheel Weiser; 2007), and *Permission to Dream Journal* (Conari Press; 2008). Lisa is passionate about getting women to write, play and collage their way to living the life of their dreams!

Lisa, her books and Femail Creations, have often been featured on television, various syndicated radio programs, and in many national magazines including: *O the Oprah Magazine*, *In Touch* magazine, *Women's Day*, and on the cover of *BusinessWeek*.

In addition to running her own companies and writing books, Lisa is a highly sought-after business consultant for companies and individuals seeking creative, merchandising, marketing or branding advice.

Lisa is a dynamic keynote speaker and workshop presenter all around the country for clients such as Eli Lilly, the National Association of Women Business Owners, and American Express.

FOR MORE INFORMATION, VISIT LISA'S POPULAR BLOG,
WITH OVER 250,000 ONLINE SUBSCRIBERS:
www.thebarefootceo.com OR **www.femailcreations.com**

BJ GALLAGHER is an inspirational author and speaker. She writes business books that educate and empower, women's books that enlighten and entertain, gift books that inspire and inform, and kids' books that charm and delight. Whether her audience is corporate executives, working women, or a group of giggling youngsters, her message is powerful, positive and practical. She motivates and teaches with empathy, understanding, and more than a little humor.

BJ's international best-seller, *A Peacock in the Land of Penguins* (Berrett-Koehler; third edition 2001), has sold over 300,000 copies in 22 languages. Her most recent books include:

~ *It's Never Too Late to Be What You Might Have Been* (Viva Editions; 2009)
~ *Why Don't I Do the Things I Know Are Good For Me?* (Berkley; 2009)
~ *Learning to Dance in the Rain* (Simple Truths; 2009)
~ *The Best Way Out is Always Through* (Simple Truths; 2009)

BJ and her books have been featured on CBS Evening News with Bob Schieffer, the Today Show with Matt Lauer, Fox News, PBS, CNN, and other television and radio programs. She is quoted almost weekly in various newspapers, women's magazines, and websites, including: *O the Oprah Magazine, Redbook, Woman's World, Ladies Home Journal, First for Women, New York Times, Chicago Tribune, Wall Street Journal, Christian Science Monitor, Orlando Sentinel, Financial Times* (U.K.), *The Guardian* (U.K.), CareerBuilder.com, MSNBC.com, CNN.com.

In addition to writing books, BJ also conducts seminars and delivers keynotes at conferences across the country. Her clients include: IBM, Chevron, U.S. Veterans Administration, John Deere Credit Canada, Volkswagen, Farm Credit Services of America, Raytheon, U.S. Department of Interior, Phoenix Newspapers Inc., the American Press Institute, Infiniti, Nissan, U.S. Army, Atlanta Journal Constitution, among others.

FOR MORE INFORMATION, VISIT BJ'S WEB SITES:
**www.womenneed2know.com   www.bjgallagher.com
www.peacockproductions.com**